# DON'T
## WORRY

A builder was walking home,
when he found a dog
in a deep hole.
"Don't worry," he said to the dog.
"I'll rescue you."

He put his ladder into the deep hole.
But it was not long enough
to reach the bottom.

2

Along came a mountain climber.
She stopped to see why the builder
was looking in the hole.
"Don't worry," she said to the builder.
"I'll rescue the dog."

She put a rope down the deep hole.
It went right to the bottom.
But the dog didn't know
how to climb up the rope.

Along came a teacher.
He stopped and looked in the hole, too.
"Don't worry," he said to the builder
and the mountain climber.
"I'm good at thinking of ideas.
I'll think of a way
to rescue the dog."

He thought for a long time.

At last, he said,
"You two will have to help me."

So the builder and the mountain climber
sat down with the teacher.
They all thought hard together.

Along came a boy with a bucket.
He looked in the hole.
He looked at the people thinking.

8

He went and filled his bucket
and poured the water into the hole.

He did it again,
and again,
and again.

The builder and the mountain climber
and the teacher
looked up and frowned.
"Little boy,
stop playing with the water.
We are thinking very hard.
We have to rescue the dog
from the deep hole."

"I know," said the boy.

While the builder
and the mountain climber
and the teacher
went on thinking,
the boy emptied another bucket of water
into the hole.

Then he emptied another,
and another,
and another.

At last, the builder jumped up.
"Little boy, get out of the way," he said.

"We have a good idea,"
said the teacher.
"The mountain climber
is going to climb down the ladder,
and then slide down the rope
and rescue the dog."

"Don't worry about the dog,"
said the boy.
"He swam out
and now he's on his way home."